SPACE EXPLORERS

DISCOVERING THE UNIVERSE

Giles Sparrow

Published in 2018 by Enslow Publishing, LLC.
101 W. 23rd Street, Suite 240, New York, NY 10011

Library of Congress Cataloging-in-Publication Data

Names: Sparrow, Giles, 1970- author.
Title: Discovering the universe / Giles Sparrow.
Description: New York, NY : Enslow Publishing, 2018. | Series: Space explorers | Audience: K to Grade 3. | Includes bibliographical references and index.
Identifiers: LCCN 2017031490| ISBN 9780766092648 (library bound) | ISBN 9780766093997 (pbk.) | ISBN 9780766094000 (6 pack)
Subjects: LCSH: Cosmology—Juvenile literature.
Classification: LCC QB983 .S663 2018 | DDC 520—dc23
LC record available at https://lccn.loc.gov/2017031490

Printed in the United States of America

To Our Readers: We have done our best to make sure all websites in this book were active and appropriate when we went to press. However, the author and the publisher have no control over and assume no liability for the material available on those websites or on any websites they may link to. Any comments or suggestions can be sent by e-mail to customerservice@enslow.com.

Picture Credits:
Key: b-bottom, t-top, c-center, l-left, r-right ESO: 13br (Swinburne Astronomy Productions); Getty Images: 8-9 & 26tr (Ann Ronan Pictures/Print Collector), 10-11 (Roger Ressmeyer/Corbis/VCG); Max-Planck-Institut für extraterrestrische Physik: 21b; NASA: 6-7 & 26t, 6b, 7tr, 14bl (NRAO/AUI/NSF/STScI/JPL-Caltech), 14c, 15bl (Caltech, UC Berkeley, Albert Einstein Institute, Perimeter Institute for Theoretical Physics, National Science Foundation/Blue Waters), 15bc & 26bl (JPL-Caltech), 15br (JPL-Caltech/K Gordon, ASU), 20-21, 20br & 27cl, 23cr & 27cr, 23bl, 24br & 27bl, 29tl, 29bl; Shutterstock: cover & title page main (Vadim Sadovski), tl (Nicku), cl (Josef Pittner), bl (3Dsculptor), c (Thanapun), br (Christina Krivonos), 4-5 (Stefano Garau), 4cl & 31bl (MaraQu), 4b (Viktar Malyshchyts), 4cr & 30t (NASA), 5t & 31br (tose), 5br &31tr (pixbox77), 7br (Timothy Hodgkinson/NASA), 8l (Zbiq), 9r (iryna1), 10b & 26cr (Georgios Kollidas/R Hart), 11tr (VectorPot), 11cr (BlueRingMedia), 11br (Olga Rutko), 12-13 & 26br (EastVillage Images), 14-15 (Mopic), 15c (Designua), 16-17, 17tr (NASA), 17br & 27 tl (bhjary), 18-19 (IrinaK), 18br & 27tr (Jennifer Stone), 19tr (Zern Liew), 22-23 (Vadim Sadovski/NASA), 23tr (bhjary), 24-25 (edobric), 28tr (Liubov Fediashova), 28bl (Vadim Sadovski), 29cr (AstroStar); Wikimedia Commons: 9bl (Micheltb), 12c (z2amiller), 16cr (Lemuel Francis Abbott/National Portrait Gallery, UK), 19r (Arecibo Observatory).

Enslow Publishing
101 W. 23rd Street
Suite 240
New York, NY 10011
USA
enslow.com

CONTENTS

Introduction.. 4

Space.. 6

Early Ideas.. 8

Telescopes 10

Giant Telescopes...................................... 12

The Electromagnetic Spectrum............... 14

Infrared Telescopes 16

Radio Astronomy 18

Special Rays 20

Hubble Space Telescope 22

Space Observatories 24

Did You Know?.. 26

Your Questions Answered........................ 28

Glossary 30

Further Information 31

Index.. 32

Introduction

Our Universe is a huge area of space made up of everything we can see in every direction. It contains a great number of different objects—from tiny specks of cosmic dust to mighty galaxy superclusters. The most interesting of these are planets, stars and nebulae, galaxies, and clusters of galaxies.

Stars

A star is a dense (tightly packed) ball of gas that shines through chemical reactions in its core (middle). Our Sun is a star. Stars range from red dwarfs, much smaller and fainter than the Sun, to supergiants a hundred times larger and a million times brighter.

Planets

A planet is a large ball of rock or gas that orbits (travels around) a star. In our solar system there are eight "major" planets, several dwarf planets, and countless smaller objects. These range from asteroids and comets down to tiny specks of dust.

Nebulae

The space between the stars is filled with mostly unseen clouds of gas and dust called nebulae. Where they collapse (fall in) and grow dense enough to form new stars, they light up from within.

Galaxies

A galaxy is a huge cloud of stars, gas, and dust, including nebulae, held together by a force called gravity. There are many different types of galaxy. This is because their shape, the nature of their stars, and the amount of gas and dust within them can vary.

This is our home galaxy, the Milky Way, seen from Earth. Our view of the Universe depends on what we can see using the best technologies that we have.

Galaxy Clusters

Gravity makes galaxies bunch together to form clusters that are millions of light-years wide. These clusters join together at the edges to form even bigger superclusters—the largest structures in the Universe.

Space

Outer space is not far away—in fact, it starts just 60 miles (100 km) above your head. That is where scientists and pilots place the "edge of space"—the region where Earth's air fades away to nothing, and where people need spacesuits and spacecraft to survive.

Solar panels fitted to the service module make electricity in space. The service module is behind the crew capsule.

Outside Earth's atmosphere, conditions switch suddenly between freezing darkness and blazing sunlight.

Weightless in Orbit

Most spacecraft and astronauts work in a region called Low Earth Orbit (LEO), where they fly around our planet at a fast enough speed to cancel out the downward pull of Earth's gravity. This means that astronauts on board an orbiting spacecraft float around in weightless conditions, free from the effects of gravity.

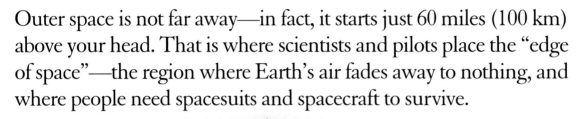

Spacecraft operate in an airless type of space called a vacuum.

Astronaut Chris Hadfield relaxes on board the *International Space Station*, which is in LEO.

SPACECRAFT PROFILE

Name: *Orion*
Launch date: 2023 (planned)
Height: 11 ft (3.3 m)
Diameter: 16 ft (5 m)
Weight: 57,000 lb (25,800 kg)
Crew size: 4 people
Launch vehicle: NASA SLS

Crew module protects up to four astronauts from the dangers of space.

Orion flew on its first unmanned test launch in 2014.

Lost in Space

Early spacecraft did not get far enough away from Earth to see our whole planet afloat in space. The first people to do this were the crew of *Apollo 8*, who flew all the way to the Moon and back in December 1968. The pictures they took showed for the first time how tiny and fragile our planet is, and moved people to start taking better care of it.

Images taken in space are used to study Earth's changing climate.

NASA's *Orion* spacecraft is made to carry astronauts into Earth's orbit and to nearby space objects.

Early Ideas

People have looked up at the stars and planets, and tried to explain them, since before written history. Many believed that these strange lights in the sky could control events on Earth, and they tried to foresee their movements. This was the birth of astronomy.

Greek Astronomers

The ancient Greeks were the first people to come up with complete models of the Universe, in the last few centuries BCE. Believing that Earth was the biggest and most important object, they put it in the middle of space, with everything else moving around it.

Native peoples of Central and South America built huge stone temples in places that lined them up with the stars and planets in the night sky.

The Greek astronomer Hipparchus realized that the Earth was tilted on its axis.

Before the invention of telescopes, astronomers used instruments such as this armillary sphere.

A Solar System

The idea of Earth in the middle of everything lasted almost 2,000 years, even though astronomers found it did not help them work out the movement of planets. In 1514, Polish priest Nicolaus Copernicus suggested that the Sun was actually at the heart of our solar system, and Earth was just one of many planets moving around it.

Armillary spheres help to measure where objects are in the sky.

Copernicus's ideas were not proven until the early 1600s.

Signs of the Zodiac

Ancient astronomers made pictures out of the stars in the sky—the patterns that we call constellations. They soon noticed that the Sun and planets followed paths around the sky that moved through just 12 of these constellations, so they gave these special importance. They became the signs of the zodiac.

Most of the zodiac constellations are animals.

Telescopes

Telescopes are the most important tools astronomers use to look at objects in space. They gather up much more light than our human eyes so that we can see fainter objects, and they create a magnified (blown-up) image so that we can see much smaller details.

Two Designs

Telescopes come in two types. Refractors use two or more lenses at either end of a long tube to create a magnified image. Reflectors use a mirror to reflect light to a lens, and can have a more compact design. The job of the first lens or mirror is to collect light from a large area and bend or reflect it so that it passes through the smaller eyepiece lens.

The Yerkes Observatory refractor is the world's largest successful lens-based telescope.

Birth of the Telescope

The first telescopes were made by Dutch lensmakers around 1608, but the invention was made famous by Italian astronomer Galileo Galilei, who built his own telescope a few months later. He used it to make important discoveries, studying the moons around Jupiter, craters on the Moon, and star clouds in the Milky Way.

Galilei's studies made him believe that the planets move around the Sun, as Copernicus had suggested.

TELESCOPE PROFILE

Name: Yerkes refractor
Built: 1897
Lens diameter: 40 in (102 cm)
Length: 63 ft (19.2 m)
Weight: 26 tons (23.5 tonnes)
Location: Williams Bay, Wisconsin, U.S.A.

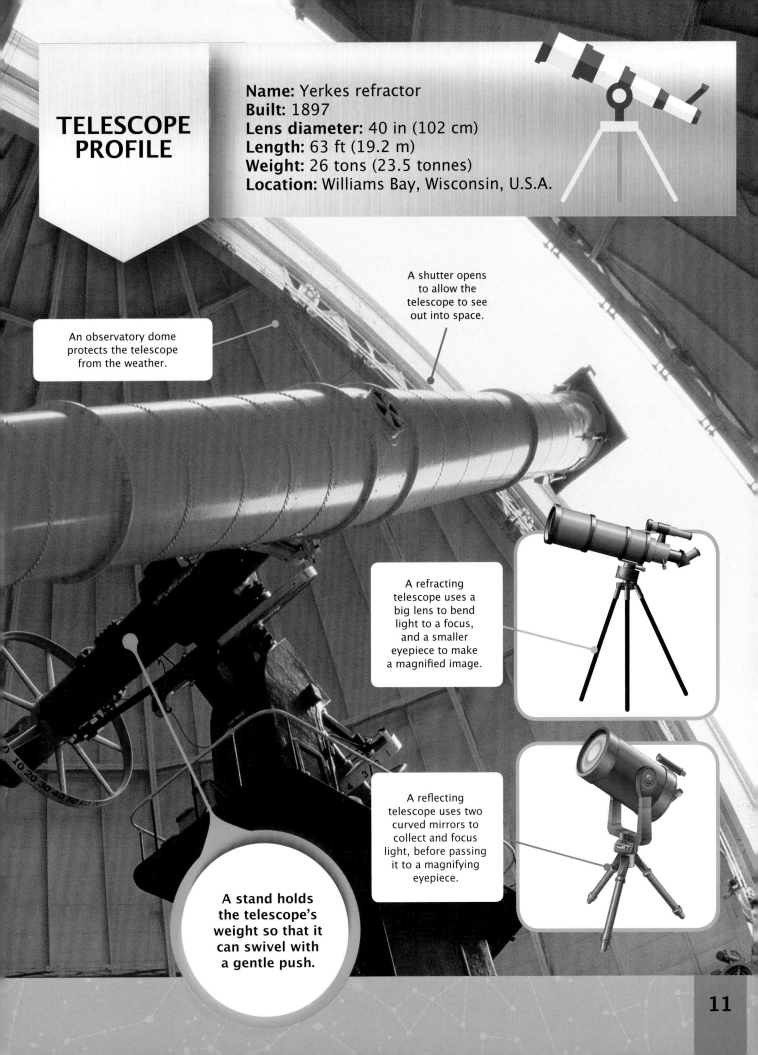

A shutter opens to allow the telescope to see out into space.

An observatory dome protects the telescope from the weather.

A refracting telescope uses a big lens to bend light to a focus, and a smaller eyepiece to make a magnified image.

A reflecting telescope uses two curved mirrors to collect and focus light, before passing it to a magnifying eyepiece.

A stand holds the telescope's weight so that it can swivel with a gentle push.

Giant Telescopes

Today's largest telescopes are all reflectors. They use huge mirrors to collect enormous amounts of light, but astronomers don't look through them directly—instead of an eyepiece, they direct their light into electronic detectors that can reveal any hidden details.

Many Mirrors

Instead of using a single mirror, many modern telescopes use many hexagonal (six-sided) mirror pieces, set together in a honeycomb pattern. Their position and shape can be changed by computer-controlled motors as the telescope swings to look in different directions. A single mirror might bend out of shape under its own weight.

The Canada–France–Hawaii Telescope (CFHT) has a single 11.8 ft (3.6-m) mirror. Its camera takes some of the largest pictures of the sky.

Today's large telescopes are built on high mountains that put them above most of Earth's weather and atmosphere.

The back of the Keck Telescope shows its many mirrors.

TELESCOPE PROFILE

Name: Gemini Telescopes
Built: 1999 and 2000
Mirror diameters: 26.9 ft (8.2 m)
Mirror weights: 22 tons (20 tonnes)
Locations: Mauna Kea, Hawaii and Cerro Pachon, Chile

Gemini North is an 8.2–m (26.9–ft) telescope in Hawaii. It has an identical twin, Gemini South, in Chile.

Vents in the dome help to keep the telescope cool during the day.

The E–ELT's mirror is made up of 798 hexagonal segments.

Under Construction

Future telescopes will dwarf even today's monsters. When complete in 2024, the European Extremely Large Telescope (E-ELT) will have a mirror that is an incredible 129 ft (39.3 m) across.

The Electromagnetic Spectrum

Scientists call the light we see with our eyes a form of electromagnetic radiation—a pattern of electric and magnetic waves moving through space at the speed of light. Light is just one small part of a much wider electromagnetic spectrum, and different objects release different kinds of radiation.

The wavelength of red light is almost twice as long as that of blue light.

Wavelength and Frequency

All kinds of electromagnetic radiation move at the speed of light—the differences between them are because of their wavelength (the length of individual waves) and frequency (the number of waves that pass a fixed point every second). The shorter the wavelength and higher the frequency, the more energy a wave can carry.

Planets "shine" by reflecting the light of their stars. The wavelength they reflect can show the chemistry of their atmospheres.

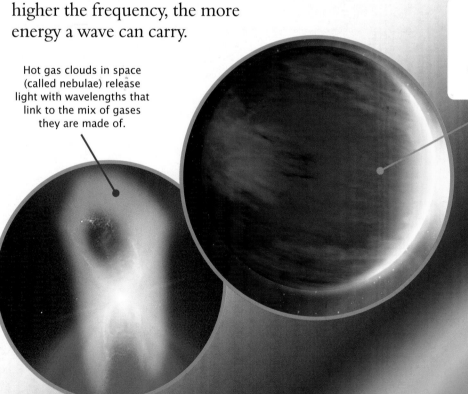

Hot gas clouds in space (called nebulae) release light with wavelengths that link to the mix of gases they are made of.

The prism slows down blue light more than red light.

A glass prism bends light by different amounts depending on its wavelength.

A beam of sunlight contains a many different wavelengths.

Astronomers split the spectrum into regions depending on the amount of energy carried in different waves.

WAVELENGTHS

FREQUENCY

VISIBLE SPECTRUM

GAMMA RAYS | X-RAYS | ULTRAVIOLET | INFRARED | MICROWAVES | RADIO WAVES

High-energy gamma rays are released only by violent cosmic events, such as exploding stars.

X-rays are high-energy rays that are released by superhot gas at million-degree temperatures.

Infrared radiation carries less energy than visible light, and is released by cool space objects.

Infrared Telescopes

Objects that are too cold to shine in visible light can still send out a lot of infrared or heat radiation. Almost everything on Earth glows in the infrared, but so do other planets, and the clouds of gas and dust from which stars are born.

Finding Infrared

In order to find the faint infrared radiation from distant space objects, astronomers need to try to block out all the radiation from Earth and even from the telescope itself. This is why infrared telescopes are built on high, cold mountaintops or—even better—launched into space as satellites.

Discovery by Accident

Infrared was the first invisible radiation to be discovered, in 1800. It was found by chance by astronomer William Herschel, during an experiment to measure the temperatures of blue, yellow, and red sunlight. Herschel split light through a prism into a rainbow-like spectrum, but discovered that the temperature was hottest just beyond the red end of this spectrum, where no light can be seen.

As well as infrared, William Herschel is famous for discovering the planet Uranus in 1781.

Winds from newborn stars blow the gas around.

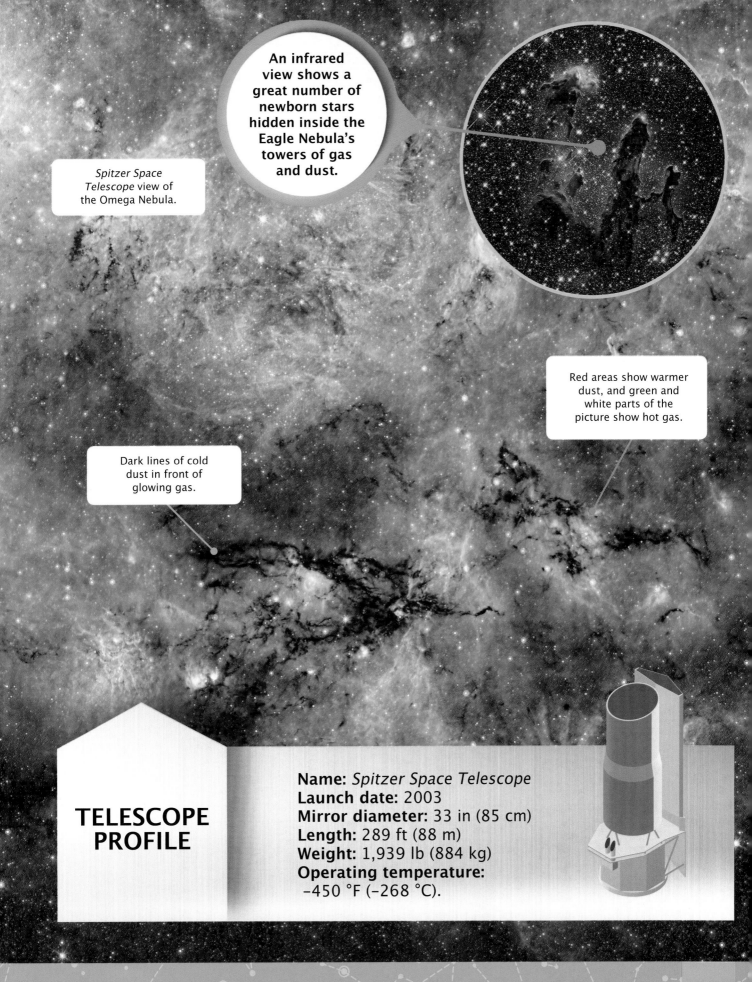

An infrared view shows a great number of newborn stars hidden inside the Eagle Nebula's towers of gas and dust.

Spitzer Space Telescope view of the Omega Nebula.

Red areas show warmer dust, and green and white parts of the picture show hot gas.

Dark lines of cold dust in front of glowing gas.

TELESCOPE PROFILE

Name: Spitzer Space Telescope
Launch date: 2003
Mirror diameter: 33 in (85 cm)
Length: 289 ft (88 m)
Weight: 1,939 lb (884 kg)
Operating temperature: −450 °F (−268 °C).

Radio Astronomy

Radio waves are the longest, lowest-energy type of electromagnetic radiation, released by some of the coldest objects in the Universe. They help astronomers to find clouds of hydrogen that shape our galaxy and others.

Giant Dishes

Radio wavelengths are millions of times longer than visible light—so spread out that it is hard to work out where they are coming from. So astronomers build giant radio telescopes—metal dishes that collect waves across a huge surface before measuring them with sensitive electronics.

The Very Large Array in New Mexico combines the signals from 27 dishes to create radio pictures of the sky.

Biggest Dishes

The largest single-dish radio telescope used to be an enormous 1,000-ft (300-m) instrument at Arecibo in Puerto Rico. This huge "detector horn" was hung from cables high above the dish. In 2016, Arecibo was overtaken by FAST, an even larger telescope at Dawodang in southern China. It is an amazing 1,600 ft (500 m) across.

The Arecibo Telescope in Puerto Rico

TELESCOPE PROFILE

Name: Very Large Array
Built: 1973–80
Location: Socorro, New Mexico, U.S.A.
Dish diameter: 85 x 82 ft (27 x 25 m)
Weight: 460,000 lb (209,000 kg) each
Track length: 13 miles (3 x 21 km)

Signals from each telescope are combined using a method called interferometry.

In 1974, scientists used the giant Arecibo dish to beam this radio message at a distant star cluster. It is a picture message addressed to any extraterrestrial life (aliens).

The elements that make up human DNA

DNA, which is found in the cells of our body. Our DNA tells our cells how to grow.

Human beings

Solar system (Earth is third planet from the Sun)

Arecibo radio telescope

Dishes can be moved along the Y-shaped track by a special machine.

Special Rays

Electromagnetic waves with more energy than visible light are mostly stopped by Earth's atmosphere. This is good for life on Earth, because these rays can be dangerous to humans and animals. But it is a problem for astronomers.

Sunrise is a telescope with a 1-m (40-in) mirror, made to study the Sun's ultraviolet rays.

Types of Ray

There are three types of high-energy rays. Those closest to visible light are called ultraviolet (UV) rays, and are released by many objects including the Sun. Those with higher energy are called X-rays and gamma rays. These are created only by the hottest objects and most violent events in the Universe.

Gamma-Ray Bursts

The strongest gamma rays from space come in sudden bursts, and astronomers are still trying to work out where they come from. One kind of gamma-ray burst may come from huge supernova explosions that happen during the death of massive stars. Other, much shorter bursts could be created when superdense neutron stars or black holes come together.

Some supernova explosions may shoot out thin beams of gamma rays.

A helium–filled weather balloon lifted *Sunrise* more than 19 miles (30 km) high, where a lot of UV hasn't been stopped by Earth's atmosphere yet.

The *Sunrise* UV telescope is strapped to a balloon. It carried out two missions, in June 2009 and June 2013.

Solar panel makes energy to power the telescope.

X-rays from the Sun reflected off the Moon.

Both *Sunrise* missions were launched from the Esrange Space Center in northern Sweden. It is in the Arctic Circle where, during summertime, the Sun never sets.

Hubble Space Telescope

The most successful telescope ever built, the *Hubble Space Telescope* (*HST*) was the first large visible-light telescope ever put into space. From where it is above Earth's atmosphere, it has the clearest and sharpest views of the Universe.

HST has four bays for carrying many different cameras and other measuring instruments.

Radio antennae connect *HST* with its controllers on Earth using other satellites.

A special tube keeps the mirror safe from direct sunlight and extreme temperature changes.

Hubble has been repaired and upgraded by five space shuttle missions during its lifetime. The last was in 2009.

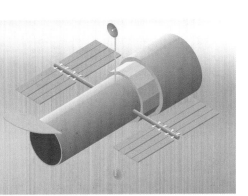
Clever Design

Sent into space in 1990, the *Hubble Space Telescope* is still working with up-to-date technology more than 25 years later. This is because it has a flexible design, with instrument units that can be replaced (removed, so that a newer unit can take its place) and upgraded. The telescope was named after the American astronomer Edwin Hubble.

An astronaut replaces one of *HST*'s instruments.

Solar panels make 1,200 watts of electricity to power the telescope and its instruments.

Discoveries

The *Hubble Space Telescope* has made many important discoveries. It has shown how stars are born in close-up for the first time, helped to discover some of the biggest stars and most distant galaxies in the Universe, and measured the speed at which our Universe is expanding (growing larger). Above all, it has taken amazing images that have forever changed the way we see space.

A *Hubble* image of the Arches, a giant star cluster near the middle of the Milky Way.

23

Space Observatories

The *HST* is the most famous space telescope, but there are many others. Earth's atmosphere blocks out almost all radiation apart from visible light and radio waves, so if astronomers want to study the Universe at these other wavelengths, they need to do it from orbit.

Benefits and Problems

Nearly all kinds of radiation can be measured better from outside Earth's atmosphere. Space telescopes can collect huge amounts of information. However, being so far from Earth is also a problem. When space telescopes break down, they are usually just left. The *HST* is the only telescope in orbit that has been repaired with the help of a service mission.

Staring at the Stars

Another good thing about having telescopes in orbit is that they do not have to stop observing during daytime. This was useful for *Kepler*, a NASA satellite launched in 2009 to search for planets around other stars. *Kepler*'s camera was designed to watch a single star cloud in the constellation Cygnus non-stop for many years. It was looking for the dips in starlight that happen if a planet passes in front of its star. This mission could only be carried out in space.

So that it can stay pointing in the same direction in space, *Kepler* orbits the Sun rather than the Earth.

A huge sun shield will protect the *JWST*'s main mirror.

The *James Webb Space Telescope* (*JWST*) will be the biggest telescope ever put into space.

The 18 pieces of gold-coated mirror will unfold once the telescope reaches orbit.

Temperatures on the underside will reach 185 °F (85 °C).

TELESCOPE PROFILE

Name: *James Webb Space Telescope*
Launch date: 2018 (planned)
Mirror diameter: 21 ft (6.5 m)
Length: 69.5 ft (21.2 m)
Weight: 13,600 lb (6,200 kg)
Operating temperature: –389 to –447 °F
 (–223 to –266 °C)

Did You Know?

There's always more to learn out about what lies in the vastness of space. Boost your knowledge with these amazing facts about the discovery of our universe.

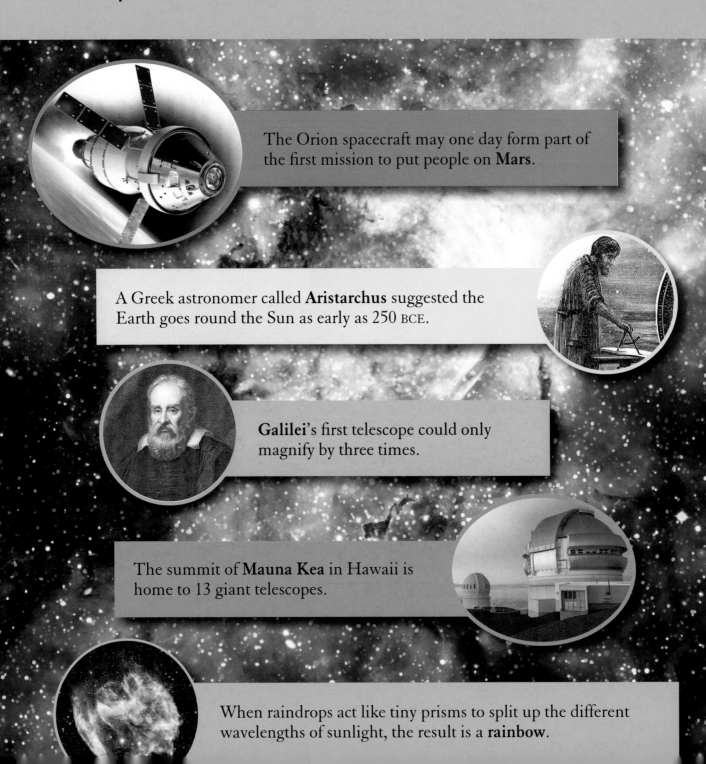

The Orion spacecraft may one day form part of the first mission to put people on **Mars**.

A Greek astronomer called **Aristarchus** suggested the Earth goes round the Sun as early as 250 BCE.

Galilei's first telescope could only magnify by three times.

The summit of **Mauna Kea** in Hawaii is home to 13 giant telescopes.

When raindrops act like tiny prisms to split up the different wavelengths of sunlight, the result is a **rainbow**.

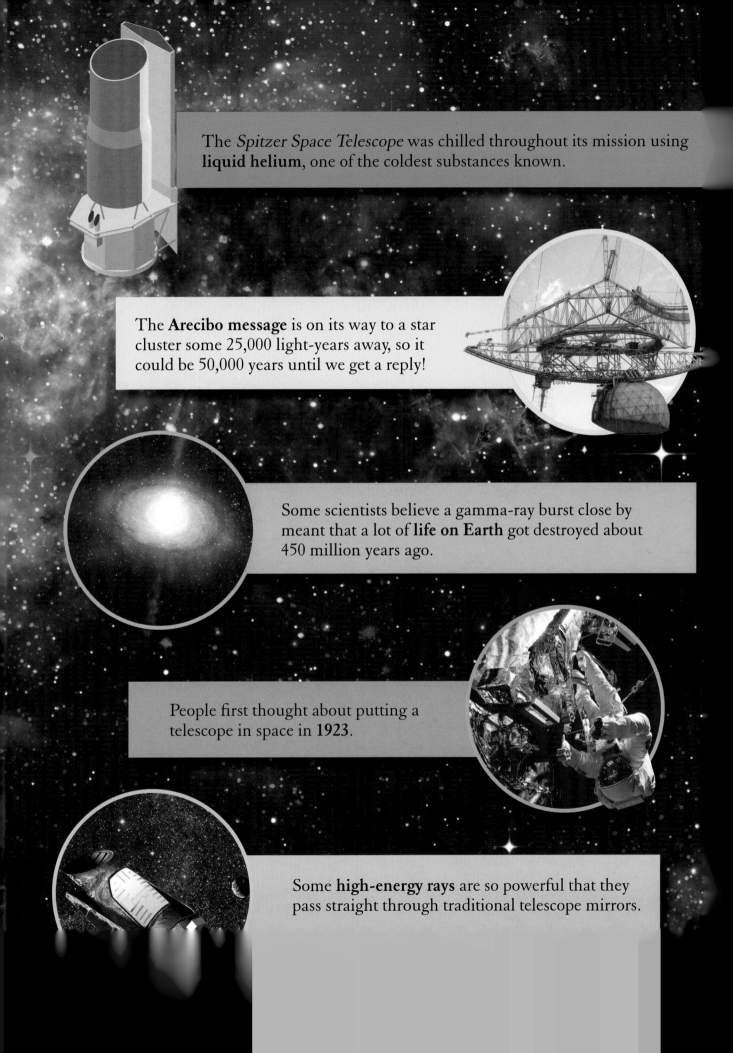

The *Spitzer Space Telescope* was chilled throughout its mission using **liquid helium**, one of the coldest substances known.

The **Arecibo message** is on its way to a star cluster some 25,000 light-years away, so it could be 50,000 years until we get a reply!

Some scientists believe a gamma-ray burst close by meant that a lot of **life on Earth** got destroyed about 450 million years ago.

People first thought about putting a telescope in space in **1923**.

Some **high-energy rays** are so powerful that they pass straight through traditional telescope mirrors.

Your Questions Answered

Scientists now know an incredible amount about our universe, but space is still bursting with amazing information and there are always more questions to be answered. This is what makes people want to become scientists and astronauts, and to study space. Here are the answers to some interesting questions about space, then you can start asking more!

Who built the first spacecraft?

The Vostok 1 spacecraft was built by a Russian team under the direction of Sergei Korolev. The Vostok 1 was the first manned spacecraft. In 1961 it was piloted by Yuri Gagarin, who became the first man in space.

How can I become an astronaut?

It's a long road so the first thing you'll need is determination, and after that, a lot of hard work.

To apply for a space program with NASA or the ESA, you need to have a good degree—in science, engineering or maths—and be in tip-top physical condition. Added to this you will need experience—pilots, for example, will need 1,000 hours in a fast jet. Alongside this is the ability to stay calm in emergency situations.

What does no-gravity feel like?

Gravity stops affecting astronauts as soon as the spacecraft enters orbit and the rocket engines are switched off. Without gravity, astronauts feel weightless. They float in the air when not strapped in with seatbelts and can move heavy objects easily. However, without gravity the blood in the body flows toward the head, which can cause headaches.

Can I look at space from home?

Yes, here are some tips to getting started with space observation.
- Start by using your own eyes. Go outside on clear nights, and start to familiarize yourself with the shapes that stars make. It will take your eyes some time to adjust to the dark.
- Buy a planisphere. This is a device that works as a guide to what you will see in the night sky on each day of the year.
- Contact your local astronomy club or astronomical society to see what they get up to and how you can get involved.

What makes a star explode?

When a star explodes, it is called a supernova. There are two reasons why this might happen. Firstly, it can happen at the end of a star's life span. As the star runs out of fuel, the core collapses and causes the explosion. Secondly, a supernova can happen when two stars share an orbit. If matter is transferred from one star to the other, having too much matter will make the star explode.

How much does it cost to build a telescope?

It varies according to the size of the telescope. The FAST telescope in China reportedly cost £140 million (about $180 million)!

Glossary

asteroid A small rocky object made up of material left over from the birth of the solar system.

atmosphere A shell of gases kept around a planet, star, or other object by its gravity.

black hole A superdense point in space, usually formed by a collapsed core of a giant star. A black hole's gravity is so powerful that even light cannot escape from it.

comet A chunk of rock and ice from the edge of the solar system. Close to the Sun, its melting ices form a coma and a tail.

constellation A star pattern in the sky and the area around it.

electromagnetic radiation A type of energy that travels at the speed of light. Radiations are given different names depending on the amount of energy they carry, from low-energy radio waves, through infrared, visible light, ultraviolet, and X-rays, to the highest-energy gamma rays.

galaxy A large system of stars, gas, and dust with anything from millions to trillions of stars.

gravity A natural force created around objects with mass, which draws other objects toward them.

light-year The distance covered by light in a year—about 9.5 trillion km (5.9 trillion miles).

Milky Way Our home galaxy, a spiral with a bar across its core. Our solar system is about 28,000 light-years from the monster black hole at its heart.

Moon Earth's closest companion in space, a ball of rock that orbits Earth every 27.3 days. Most other planets in the solar system have moons of their own.

nebula A cloud of gas or dust floating in space. Nebulae are the raw material used to make stars.

neutron star The core of a supermassive star, left behind by a supernova explosion and collapsed to the size of a city. Many neutron stars are also pulsars.

orbit A fixed path taken by one object in space around another because of the effect of gravity.

planet A world that orbits the Sun, which has enough mass and gravity to pull itself into a balllike shape, and clear space around it of other large objects.

red dwarf A small, faint star with a cool red surface and less than half the mass of the Sun.

satellite Any object orbiting a planet. Moons are natural satellites made of rock and ice. Artificial (manmade) satellites are machines in orbit around Earth.

spacecraft A vehicle that travels into space.

spectrum The spread-out band of light with different hues, created by passing light through a prism or similar device.

supernova An enormous explosion marking the death of a star much more massive than the Sun.

telescope A device that collects light or other radiations from space and uses them to create a bright, clear image. Telescopes can use either a lens or a mirror to collect light.

zodiac Twelve constellations surrounding the Sun's yearly path around Earth's sky. The planets and Moon are usually found within these constellations.

Further Information

BOOKS

Daynes, Katie. *See Inside Space.* London, UK: Usborne Publishing, 2008.

DK Reference. *Space!* New York, NY: DK Publishing, 2015.

Murphy, Glenn. *Space: The Whole Whizz-Bang Story* (Science Sorted). New York, NY: Macmillan Children's Books, 2013.

Newman, Ben. *Professor Astro Cat's Frontiers of Space.* London, UK: Flying Eye Books, 2013.

Ridley, Sarah. *Nicolaus Copernicus* (Super Scientists). New York, NY: Franklin Watts, 2016.

Rogers, Simon. *Information Graphics: Space.* Somerville, MA: Big Picture Press, 2015.

WEBSITES

www.nasa.gov/kidsclub/index.html
Join Nebula at NASA Kids' Club to play games and learn about space.

www.ngkids.co.uk/science-and-nature/ten-facts-about-space
Get started with these ten great facts about space, then explore the rest of the National Geographic Kids site for more fun.

www.esa.int/esaKIDSen/
Explore this site from the European Space Agency.
There's information, games, and news.

Index

A
aliens 19
ancient Greeks 8
Aristarchus 26
asteroids 4
astronauts 6, 7, 28
astronomers 8, 9, 10, 12, 15,
    16, 20
astronomy 8

B
black holes 20

C
comets 4
constellations 9
Copernicus, Nicolaus 9, 10
cosmic dust 4

D
dwarf planet 4

E
electromagnetic radiation 14
Esrange Space Center,
    Sweden 21

G
Gagarin, Yuri 28
galaxy 4, 23
galaxy superclusters 4, 5
Galilei, Galileo 10, 26
gamma rays 14, 15, 20, 27
gravity 5, 6, 29

H
Herschel, William 16
Hipparchus 8

Hubble, Edwin 23

I
infrared 15, 16–17
International Space Station 6

K
Kepler Satellite 24
Korolev, Sergei 28

M
Milky Way 5, 10, 23
Moon 7, 10

N
nebulae 4, 14, 17
    Eagle Nebula 17
    Omega Nebula 17
neutron stars 20

P
planets 4, 9, 10, 14
    Jupiter 10
    Mars 26
    Uranus 16

R
radio waves 18–19
red dwarf 4

S
solar system 4, 9, 19
spacecraft 6
    Apollo 7
    Orion 6, 7, 26
    Vostok 1 28
stars 4, 8, 9, 14, 15, 16, 17,
    20, 23, 24, 29

Sun 4, 9, 19, 20, 21, 24, 26
supergiants 4
supernova 20, 29

T
telescopes 9, 10–11, 12–13, 18,
    20, 21, 24, 26, 27
    Arecibo Telescope 18, 19
    Canada-France-Hawaii
        Telescope (CFHT) 12
    European Extremely Large
        Telescope (E-ELT) 13
    FAST Telescope 18, 29
    Gemini Telescopes 12, 13
    Hubble Space Telescope 22–23
    James Webb Space Telescope 25
    Keck Telescope 12
    Spitzer Space Telescope 17, 27
    Sunrise Telescope 20, 21
    Very Large Array 18

U
ultraviolet (UV) rays 14, 15, 20, 21

W
weightlessness 6

X
X-rays 14, 15, 20

Y
Yerkes Observatory 10

Z
zodiac 9